Completely Splattered

A String of Poems for the Fallen

Completely

Splattered

A String of Poems for the Fallen

By Emily Hodson

Photo taken by Emily Hodson

Forest Knows Best

June 7th, 2012

Dark, narrow and hungry,

The forest waits patiently for the girl who seeks it.

Cold, weary and naïve,

The girl knows nothing of the forest's intentions.

Fast, terrified and aware,

A rabbit runs out, trying to warn and change the girl's fate.

Lost, eager and brave,

The girl makes her way into the pit of a darkness that will never fall.

Sharp, hidden and small,

A berry bush pricks the girl's finger, letting her blood shower its delicate leaves.

Panicked, injured and alone,

The girl hears a wolf cry out from the back of a darkness that never falls.

Starving, thirsty and distracted,

The wolf tracks down the girl's scent, the scent of innocence and loneliness.

Fast, quick and intelligently,

The injured girl hides inside of a small cave, watching the wolf prowl through the forest of the darkness that never falls.

The girl is not only running from the wolf, but other predators of the night.

She is running from the ones she fears, and the ones she loves the most.

She runs from a life that was filled with menacing and evil things, things that could eventually drag her down, further than the darkness she has already encountered.

This girl just wants an escape. She wants to get lost in the forest to release her from a world where the darkness never falls.

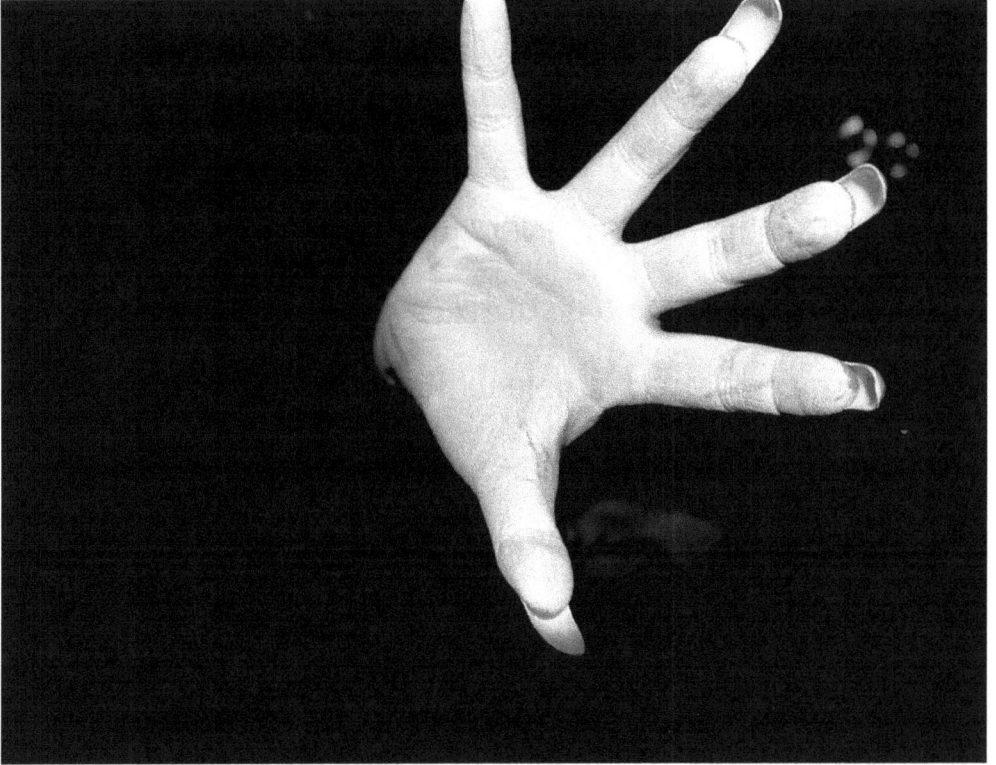

Photo taken by Sylvia Mead

Forever Cold Blooded

August 4th, 2012

The wind whistles softly in her ears as the snow lightly brushes her porcelain face.

It's cold tonight, like it is every waking, heart-stopping day.

It welcomes her skin, in a subtly frozen embrace.

The trees are painted in pale white powders of frost.

They sprinkle the living as they pass by each day.

Sleeping under the tree will only come with a high price.

For the winters are brutal and poor souls never find their way.

Once they explore here, it's only fate that decides;

Live or die, Mother Nature chooses if they stay or go.

Out in the cold and deserted mountains,

No one ever quite knows what will happen to them,

Not even the cold bloods.

The people who have always lived in this monstrous place,

Know that only the strong will survive in this creeping Death Valley filled with icicles.

When you live in the deserted parts of Alaska, even as a forever cold blooded, danger will always suck its way through the door.

Creatures of the night come crashing inside with a stringing mind, blood thirst hanging from their menacing lips.

The cold will send shivers of fear down your spine, straight to the core of your mouth.

Being alone in the mountains is one thing, but surviving it is the real question.

To be forever cold blooded is something that you have to be born with. Not everyone can survive the gloomy cold embrace of Alaska.

Glistening Beauty

August 25th, 2012

The birds are chirping,

the wood is chopping.

It's a beautiful day to start upon us.

Wildlife gathers around to embrace the new beginning that awaits their precious land.

The sun cracks a slight smile,

The clouds make way.

It's the day's turn to shine.

Nobody else's.

The river reflects the day's weather, glowing beneath the cleansed and healthy fish.

They are happy the new revised day has rewarded them too.

The mountains' snow is washed away with new scenery.

The roads are paved in gold around every living thing,

As people drive their way to reach the top.

The top of a beauty awaiting anyone who embraces each and every soul.

The humans join in celebration of their land's new beauty.

Even the visitors are mesmerized by this unique world's pure elegance.

The way it shines down on every living thing.

The way it takes care of the ground that excessively grows upon it.

Days like this, Mother Nature takes pride in making her place welcoming, with open arms and promise for a wonderful day to come to her people.

The Dark Ones

August 28th, 2012

Towards the corners of the pitch black empty classroom,

They're there.

When no one bothers or cares,

They stare.

On the streets and during the night,

These creatures know when to hit the light.

In your bed and in your dreams,

They're there.

When no one bothers or cares,

They stare.

In the car and on the stereo,

The shadows wait for us all through the night.

Considering each scenario,

They carefully pick where to cause the fright.

In your head, captured by the mind,

They're there.

When no one bothers or cares,

They stare.

Inside your skin and inside your mouth,

These are the secret places the monsters like to prowl.

They like the humans,

So beautiful and gullible.

Soft skin and a body ever so touchable.

When you know they're there,

But no one believes you, they're still there.

And in your darkest moments of your life,

When no one cares, when no one dares, when no one is fair, when no one shares,

They're still there and they still stare.

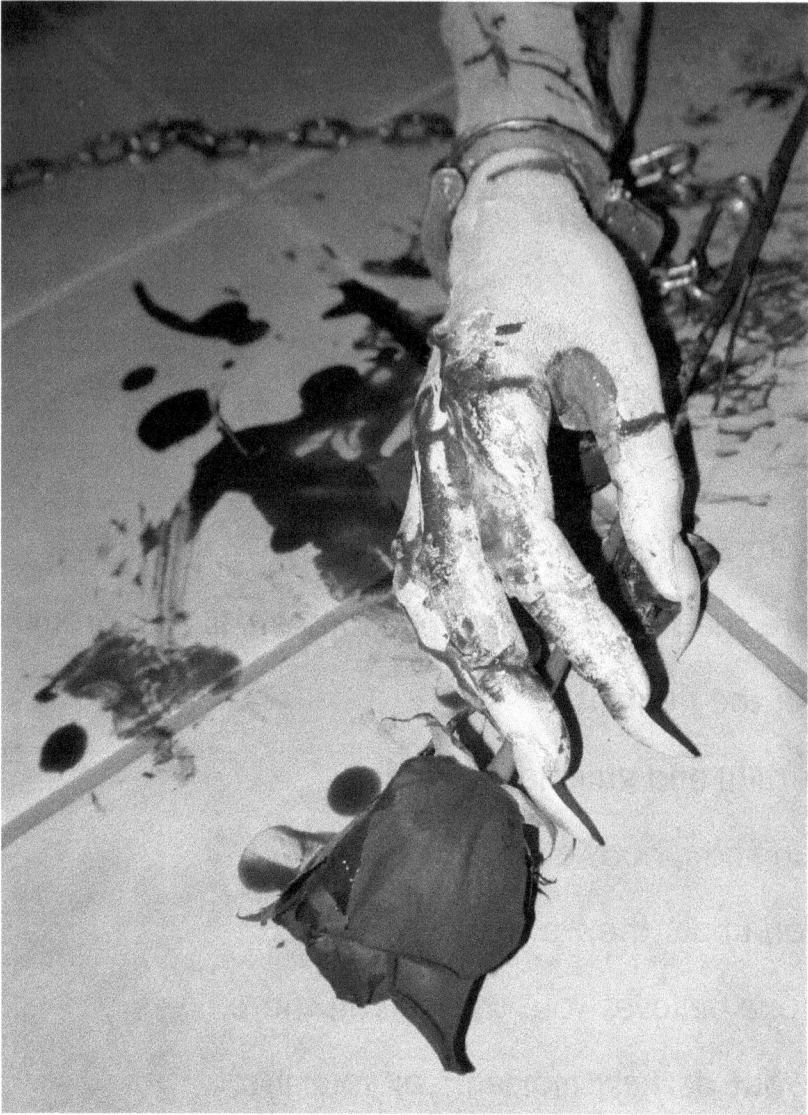

Photo taken by Sylvia Mead

He Makes Me Feel...

August 29th, 2012

Like a seed, waiting to grow into something more beautiful and rare.

In the light of his elegance, he makes me feel like a warm and comforted embrace of pillows,

Securing my doubt and worries.

He makes me feel,

Like a whole and not a half, not even just a smidge,

But a whole different person.

He makes me feel,

Like I can tell him anything.

Trust him with anything.

He is my other side and my other me.

He makes me feel,

Like a small and delicate infant, cradled and loved in his arms so securely and safely. Nothing will harm me with him.

He makes me feel,

Like a young girl, who longs for love at an innocent time in her life, hoping to ever get someone's stare.

He makes me feel,

Like a fool and an unwanted opponent for his affection.

He makes me feel,

Like my beating heart is always pumping too fast,

Every touch, every kiss,

Sends me above with warmth and air in the sky.

He makes it hard to breathe; he makes it hard to speak.

He makes me feel like the most loved person on the planet.

Photo taken by Emily Hodson

Rain Forever

August 31st, 2012

A drop here and a drop there,

Rain is essential in life, even to those who don't believe they need it.

A taste of nature's refreshing wilderness,

A helpful drop of moist to the flowers.

Rain likes to help those in need the most.

Stuck to the windshields, drenching those who stand above it,

Rain doesn't care who stands in its way.

Every touch and every taste sends shivers down spines of its true beholders.

No one can resist Rain.

The damp and refreshing air,

Fills the city in with a crisp scent of the outdoor wilderness' cleansed water and welcoming for a new beginning.

Rain works its magic in any type of setting.

It knows when the time is right.

Though the storms are brutal and sometimes traitorous,

Rain sometimes cannot control its power.

Nothing is perfect in this world and Rain takes the blame every time.

Taking the fall and hatred because of its natural instinct,

Not everyone will understand Rain and not everyone will appreciate the gifts it provides to this life.

The Never Ending Storm

September 8th, 2012

It's cold tonight, with a crisp smell of new nature, entering peoples' homes.

Something doesn't feel right as the night sends a new sort of darkness,

To the city that never trusts the weather.

No one knows what's ever going to happen as this event occasionally occurs during their least expecting times.

People have to stay close and stick together,

Once they've found out the weather has become stricken with each and every one of them.

The storm awaits patiently for its victims to arrive,

Eager to destroy at least a body or two to start.

The branches shove their way to the front of the line,

Scratching the victims' windows,

Clawing towards being the first at the taste of light.

The storm isn't getting its way though,

So it sacrifices a tree to die in spite.

Trees begin to cover buildings and houses,

Displaying their death in an unwelcoming manner.

The people fear the storm,

For it has an unstoppable power.

No one dares to leave their homes or offices,

Except for the homeless, the easiest targets for storm's thunder stick to strike first.

The storm fears them though, for they enjoy the light that shuns the storm away.

Storms are like the black sheep in the weather book.

They exist in the world but no one cares about them or acknowledges the perks it has.

No one wants them around nor needs them for any usage. Rain is about as much as they can take.

It's the last day the storm is taking any of their rubbish.

Tonight the storm seeks out for revenge.

Bully

September 10th, 2012

It's unpredictable,

In the sense that no one quite knows when it's going to happen to them.

No certain size, no certain look, they could be a next door neighbor for all you know.

Cold-hearted and cold-blooded, they hunt for the weak and only the weak.

Mostly in the night or when they think no one is looking.

They have neither rhyme nor reason, not even a trigger.

Besides the fact that they enjoy doing it,

Harming others, hurting others and even killing others,

They have no conscience when it comes to having their way with each and every oblivious victim.

They don't care what you think or what you do.

All they care about is feeling your flesh ooze between their knuckles as every punch gets more intense and brutal.

They enjoy the feel of damaging another's soul.

Destructing someone's body in the worst ways.

The thought of scaring someone to death,

Crushing their delicate feelings.

Why do they do this? You ask.

Who do they think they are? You wonder.

No one quite knows,

And no one will ever understand.

Bullies will suffer only in the end.

Karma will teach them a lesson but only with time and patience.

They will bow down to those they hurt or ruined, the day the victims become their bosses.

September 11th

September 12th, 2012

This poem is a day late,

But never a day too far from remembering what happened.

To the people who fought hard to stay alive,

This one's for you.

To the children who lost a parent or loved one,

This one's for you.

To the patrons who suffered a lifelong injury,

This one's for you.

To the victims who got their lives abruptly ripped away for no good reason at all on a regular day living,

Where no one would ever suspect this to happen,

This one's for you.

Wherever you may be after life,

You should know that we will never forget the day that

God decided to take you away from this cruel world.

You are all special and dearly reconciled and missed.

We show compassion and feel and hear your pain in our hearts every day,

The morning the devil struck his magic on a building that will never be the same again.

Though life goes on, our hearts don't as we remember the reminders of what could happen on any plane or in any airport.

Torn

October 8th, 2012

Photos taken by Sylvia Mead

In a land far away, past the mountains and trees,

Near the shimmering lake, live two princes and one delicate princess.

Two guys, one girl,

The princess can only choose one.

Which one though?

Which prince will grasp the resistant and strong-willed

heart of the princess?

Will it be Prince #1, riding on a mysterious black horse?

Though rugged in the face and less fortunate,

He can shower the princess with everlasting love and endless protection.

Or perhaps it shall be Prince #2?

Riding a healthy white horse, he offers intelligence,

Class and a wealth ahead of his young and successful life.

Prince #1 and Prince #2 are very different from each other.

The princess must choose her destiny soon,

For the time bomb is ticking and the palace can only wait for so long.

The princess wants them both though.

Each one so different than the other,

Both qualities in two princes combined,

There would be her dream man.

She wants them both and doesn't want to lose one or the other at all.

Such joy each prince brings to her heart.

"Who shall it be?"

They ask with no sympathy or compassion from the crowd.

"Prince #1 with a rugged face, poor earnings, but everlasting love?

Or Prince #2, who has good charm, wealth and intelligence to keep you happy and satisfied for a lifetime."

"Neither," she sobs. "If I can't have both, I'll let them go.

My love for them is the same. I will not choose."

The crowd grows shocked and the princess's decision is final.

Swiftly in her pink laced long dress, she lifts it slightly from the ground to run away into the forest to never return.

Prince #1 and Prince #2 both chase after her on their horses,

Ready to take on the forest that may never let them return.

Photo taken by Emily Hodson

Heart Rippers

October 10th, 2012

They travel by foot, by heels, by car.

Their hair is groomed, attained and smothered in scents of pure heaven.

One whiff of the fragrance could leave you weak in the knees for hours in one day.

They dress in a certain, particular sort of way.

A certain way that lures the male species in with just a single touch.

One...delicate...touch.

A delicate touch leading to sin, lust, and a period of embraces never ending.

Torment, betrayal, vanity, and possession,

Soon weaves into your once failed life.

They will tease you, eat you, and displease you eventually.

Once they've had enough, you're gone the next day.

They travel in packs,

And the ones that wear a little black dress will twist your mind for a century.

They'll wrap you around your finger,

Reeling you in like a fish caught in the sea.

They choose when to leave,

You choose to follow them until they

Smash your heart into a million pieces,

Like a mirror about to break into shattered glass,

Your reflection and theirs are much different,

Therefore you will learn the hard way when you

Play with poisonous fire.

Photo taken by Emily Hodson

A Land of Paradise

March 14th, 2013

As the wind passes through,

My skin and sneakers squeak as I walk.

I wonder,

The cold here is nonexistent,

But neither is the warmth.

The perfect cool breeze makes me wonder,

Is this my destiny?

My surroundings are filled with scents of freshness and new awakenings.

The people are welcoming as if they've known me my entire life.

The health and self-awareness of doing the planet a favor makes me wonder,

Is this my destiny?

Am I supposed to actually feel something inside my heart?

A feeling of acceptance and diversity circling me?

A place where it's actually okay to be me?

No such world has ever made me ever feel quite fit completely into my own shoes.

No place has ever made me fit so perfectly into a square.

It's as if I was supposed to be born here from Day 1.

My mind feels free and ready to let go of all the baggage I once carried from the past.

Ready to leave everything I know and love behind,

I walk some more.

I'm ready for my new beginning.

I'm ready for Portland.

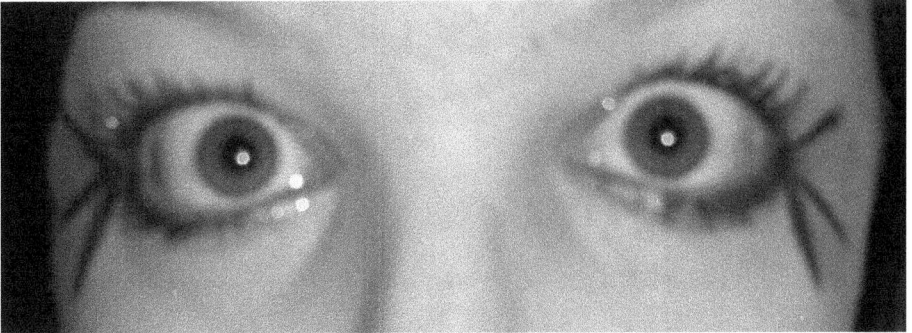

Photo taken by Emily Hodson

Silence

March 14th, 2013

His cold blue eyes are completely frozen.

They are too distracted and locked inside her doughy brown pair of innocent eyes.

Nothing can come between this very stare.

It's inseparable and neither will look away, but neither will actually speak.

Not...a...single...word.

They are both hush hush, not moving a centimeter of their eye contact away.

If it were possible, they'd never leave this gaze.

Their gaze is like a drug,

A type of trance that's difficult to escape once you lock your eyes.

They refuse to leave the site of one another's eyes.

The stare is all these two people need.

No dialogue, no touching, no thinking.

She is beautiful and he knows it.

He is strapping and she knows it.

They can't control the stare at all. It's unexplainable beyond all reasons and hard to grasp the actual reasoning.

Her dark and long hair flowing past her delicate shoulders,

Is urging to be touched by him.

His plump and ripe lips, waiting to plunge in for the signature move he so longs to make.

These are just a few examples of the procedures people do before going in for the kill.

Photo taken by Sylvia Mead

Stuck

March 14th, 2013

Her lips tremble as she enters the halls,

The halls leading to a path filled with deceit, regret and a confused beautiful mind.

Her knees shake as she rips open the cold-padded door.

In there lies a lion, ready to eat its prey,

Ready to cast its charm-like spell on his prisoner.

The girl is thrown to the bed while the King is ready to tear open his shivering prize.

She knows what she's about to get herself into though.

She knew from the very start.

There's no control or hesitance when facing the man who portrays a hungry lion.

The way his kind looks, smells and feels,

Their chiseled body and crooked smile,

Suave charm,

One touch and you'll melt your pretty little fingers off.

As the girl takes a deep, regretful breath, she lays down with her eyes closed tightly.

The Hungry lion readies himself before the ultimate kill.

He knows whose heart will be ripped out the next morning.

Something Inside

May 30th, 2013

A beat- one little beat.

One little beat turns into one larger beat.

One faster beat...One deathly beat.

A million things play in my mind as well as my skin,

How it crawls every time I encounter an episode,

This certain place that hides in the back of my mind.

Each goose bump feels like a needle in my arm, fighting to press down just a little bit further.

The more my heart beats, the more it wants to explode out of this mess I call a body.

I need an escape.

I *want* an escape.

Something is inside me.

Something I cannot explain.

It wants to get out now.

It wants to…scream.

Kill my insides and outsides from limb to limb.

This something won't get away from me.

It won't leave me alone, even with the kind words I initiate.

It'll always be a part of me,

Always inside wanting out.

But it will never respect my wishes.

Instead, it'll fill my heart with mental nightmares,

Causing it to beat a bit faster by the second.

Always making me believe the worst.

My anxiety will eventually take the best of me.

Stop. Look. Listen.

May 30th, 2013

As the wind whistles outside,

The girl slowly removes her headphones.

Her ears have grown tired of the same songs meaning nothing anymore.

On the bus, her heart for once wants to listen to all of the life she never acknowledged before.

To her right, a baby is cold, crying for a warmer blanket.

The mother is trying her best, with all the materials she has left with her.

A homeless man is fighting with the youth,

Probably wishing he could go back in time and do his life all over again.

All those decades wasted of booze and drugs.

All the pathetic money begging, theft occurrences,

Family and friend losses.

He just wants a friend.

He just wants somebody to simply talk to and maybe help his mental needs out.

A couple begins to argue.

Bills, the rent, where the relationship is going...

They're so comfortable in their pact,

They feel the whole bus needs to know about it.

The girl puts her headphones back on,

Knowing they were made for a reason:

To drown out the unstoppable flaws that never end.

Photo taken by Emily Hodson

Deceitful

May 30th, 2013

'll take what I can get for now and maybe a few months later too.

No confession or truth to the girl, just another ridiculous excuse from another ridiculous guy.

He'll move on to the next victim while the broken angel wonders what she ever did wrong to him.

Tearing apart every flaw she can think of about herself,

like why she isn't good enough, why her body isn't perfect, why her minor break outs won't ever clear her face.

He'll feel ruined because he never told her that it wasn't her with the problem, it was him.

Why he ultimately would never be good enough for a wondrous creature like herself.

"You're beautiful and gorgeous,

A real piece of artwork,"

He'll say.

"You're not like the rest,

No...no...you're different."

He'll lie.

Repeats to the same girl he'll see the next day,

Plus a maybe additional do-over next week.

"You make me smile, you're independent and I lov
about you."

He'll tell the truth, deep inside knowing he's not
enough to ever deserve this creature's affection

She's settling for less,

He thinks.

www.ingramcontent.com/pod-product-compliance
Lightning Source LLC
Chambersburg PA
CBHW060623030426

42337CB00018B/3162